D0534283

10•20•30 minute
scrapbook pages

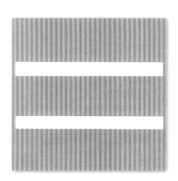

acknowledgments

©2004 by Leisure Arts, Inc., P. O. Box 55595, Little Rock, AR 72215. All rights reserved. This publication is protected under federal copyright laws. Reproduction or distribution of this publication or any other Leisure Arts publication, including publications that are out of print, is prohibited unless specifically authorized. This includes, but is not limited to, any form of reproduction on or through the Internet, including, posting, scanning, or e-mail transmission.

We have made every effort to ensure that these instruments are accurate and complete. We cannot, however, be responsible for human error, typographical mistakes, or variations in individual work.

10-20-30 Minute Scrapbook Pages is the ninth in a series of books written by NanC and Company and published by Leisure Arts, Inc.

Author: Nancy M. Hill
Design Director: Candice Snyder
Senior Editor: Candice Smoot
Graphic Designers: Rafael Nielson
                     Maren Ogden
Photographer: Julianne Smoot
Cover Design: Maren Ogden
Copy Editor: Sharon Staples

Cover Layouts: NanC and Company Design
                Tarri Botwinski

For information about sales visit the Leisure Arts web site at www.leisurearts.com

Let's face it, most of us have far more photos than we have time to scrapbook and, in many instances, we just continue to collect and inherit more photos. As you can see by this photo, I have a photographer for a husband, and even after years of scrapbooking, I can't stay on top of these photos.

If you picked up this book, you are probably what I consider a "time-challenged" scrapper. You love to scrap, but simply can't devote as much time to it as you would like. This idea book with step-by-step pictures and instructions can help you make great scrapbook pages with character and personality in 10, 20 and 30 minutes, once you have gathered your photos and supplies. The creative and simple ideas in this book are perfect for "scraplifting" onto your own pages. Enjoy seeing your collection of photos on scrapbook pages instead of hidden in their boxes and drawers.

Happy time saving,

Nancy

Go Western

SUSIE

When I was 9 years old, I took Western riding lessons at Lakeway. My horse was named Chili, and I remember thinking he was just the greatest.

Lake Travis   1973

table of contents

busch gardens

The Petting Zoo

Busch
Gardens

Tampa, Florida

Designer: NanC and Company Design

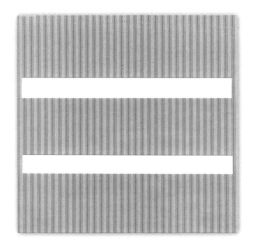

step one

Cut two 1 x 11 inch strips of white cardstock and adhere horizontally to blue patterned paper as shown. Trim blue patterned paper to just shy of 12 inches.

step two

Trim two of four 4 x 6 photos to 4 inches square. Adhere the four photos to the background as shown.

step three

Attach sticker letters onto a pre-made tag to create the title. Handwrite onto the tag and background and draw a decorative design around the white strips of cardstock and the tag. Attach background to a sheet of white cardstock with four large silver brads. Embellish the layout with white fiber.

supplies: Cardstock: DCWV; Patterned Paper: Memories in the Making; Stickers: DCWV

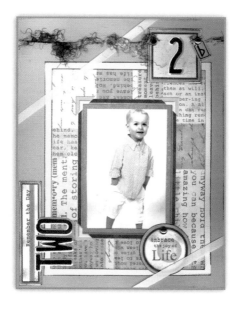

step one

Mount a photo behind a pre-made frame, mat the frame with yellow cardstock and ink the edges. Trim a sheet of green cardstock to just smaller than the finished size of the page. Adhere the matted frame to the bottom right corner of the green cardstock.

step two

Adhere two pieces of yellow ribbon to the page overlapping the corners of the photo frame.

step three

Adhere the green cardstock onto purple cardstock and ink the edges. Finish by adhering matted and inked punch-outs, letter stickers for the title and fiber to the top of the page.

supplies: Cardstock: Bazzill; Fiber: Fibers by the Yard; Metal Letter: Art Accentz by Provo Craft; Brads: Making Memories; Stickers: Sticker Studio; Frame: Carolee's Creations; Punch Outs: Carolee's Creations; Ribbon: Offray & Son, Inc.

two

Designer: Sam Cousins

paradise

Designer: NanC and Company Design

step one

step two

step three

Tear a strip out of the middle of a sheet of yellow cardstock. Adhere the yellow cardstock onto a sheet of black cardstock.

Double mat a large photo and adhere to the background.

Sand metallic letters, thread with orange and yellow floss and knot at the top. Adhere to the bottom of the photo. Complete the layout by inking the edges with black ink.

supplies: Cardstock: DCWV; Patterned Paper: Memories in the Making; Metallic Letters: DCWV; Floss: Making Memories

10

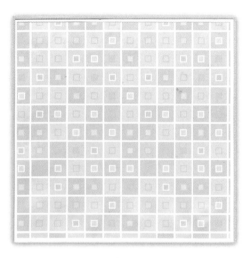

step one

Trim a sheet of yellow patterned paper and mat with white cardstock. Adhere both to a sheet of yellow cardstock.

step two

Adhere a photo to the left side of the background. Create the title directly onto the photo with rub-on letters.

step three

Frame two black and white photos with metallic frames and adhere to the background as shown.

supplies: Cardstock: DCWV; Patterned Paper: DCWV; Metallic Frame: DCWV; Rub-ons: Making Memories

treasure

Designer: Tarri Botwinski

winter

WINTER

Designer: Miranda Isenberg

step one

Adhere a silver mat vertically onto the top left corner of a sheet of cardstock. Attach a vellum quote to a photo with mini brads and adhere to the background.

step two

Punch three photos into 2-inch squares. Adhere the photos to the background as shown.

step three

Adhere gingham ribbon horizontally above and below the three photos. Attach a license plate embellishment with brads.

step four

Adhere snowflake buttons (with shanks cut off) to the background. Print journaling onto a piece of white cardstock and tuck behind the large photo with the vellum quote.

supplies: Cardstock: Bazzill; Patterned Paper: DCWV; License Plate: Junkitz; Brads: Lasting Impressions; Vellum Quote: DCWV, Buttons: Dress It Up!

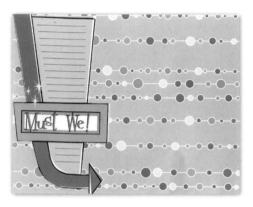

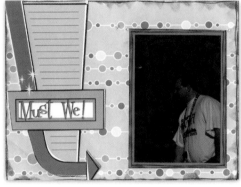

step one

Attach a journaling sticker to the left hand side of circle patterned paper.

step two

Mat a photo with green paper, ink the edges, draw a double black line around the photo on the mat and adhere to the background. Ink and draw a double black line around the entire layout.

step three

Create a subtitle by attaching stickers to a tag. Attach the tag with a brad to the top left corner of the photo. Attach three other brads to the other corners of the photo and string fiber around the brads. Complete the layout with handwritten journaling.

supplies: Patterned Paper: SEI; Tag: SEI; Fiber: Fibers by the Yard; Brads: Making Memories; Stickers: SEI

Here we go again. The 1st time we visited "Mexico" Steve saw this carving & ran up to it. He snuggled his profile close to it & said "here, take my picture." During this visit to "Mexico" he did the same thing... "here, take my picture." He thinks it (& he) are pretty funny. I have a

Must We !

a NEW Tradition

feeling this is going to be a new tradition!

Designer: Sam Cousins

glamour girls

Glamour Girls

Madison · age 7

Alexis · age 6

Bailey · age 3

2001

Designer: NanC and Company Design

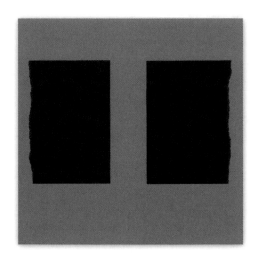

step one

Cut two mats out of black cardstock. Tear the left side of one and the right side of the other. Adhere the mats to the pink cardstock as shown.

step two

Mat three photos with light pink cardstock. Adhere two photos to the background over the black mats and one photo overlapping the bottom of the other photos. Attach letter stickers to the background for the title and date.

step three

Adhere bows to the background and handwrite names and ages below each photo. Attach an eyelet to a metallic flower, string black floss through the eyelet and hang the flower from the top bow.

supplies: Cardstock: DCWV; Patterned Paper: Memories in the Making; Metal Embellishment: Making Memories; Eyelet: Making Memories; Stickers: DCWV; Ribbon: Offray & Son, Inc.

step one

Trim a sheet of stripe patterned paper and adhere to a sheet of blue cardstock.

step two

Cut a 7½ x 8¾ inch piece of stripe patterned paper and a 2¾ x 3¼ inch piece of circle patterned paper and adhere to the background as shown.

step three

Adhere a photo and vellum quote over the blocks of patterned paper.

step four

Cut strips of blue vellum and adhere to the background in a crisscross pattern. Decoratively stitch the ends of the vellum with yellow floss. Handwrite the name and age of the child onto a premade tag. Cut out circles from the circle patterned paper. Attach the tag and circles to the background with eyelets. Finish by adorning the vellum quote with three eyelets down the left side.

supplies: Cardstock: DCWV; Patterned Paper: Memories in the Making; Vellum: Memories in the Making; Tag: Memories in the Making; Eyelets: Making Memories; Floss: Making Memories

keep smiling

keep

smiling

Zackary
age 5

Designer: NanC and Company Design

green never looked so good

St. Patrick's Day

Green never looked so good!

Designer: Miranda Isenberg

step one

Adhere two mulberry mats onto a sheet of cardstock overlapping one another as shown. Adhere one vertically and one horizontally.

step two

Mat a large photo with white cardstock and adhere to the background over the mulberry mats. Adhere additional photos at an angle below the large photo.

step three

Adhere a ribbon horizontally to the background over the bottom photos. Complete the layout by adhering a vellum quote and shamrock embellishments to the background and by attaching photo anchors to the large photo.

supplies: Cardstock: Bazzill; Mulberry Paper: DCWV; Brads: Lasting Impressions; Photo Anchors: Making Memories; Shamrock Embellishment: Sarah Heidt; Vellum Quote: DCWV

10

step one

Mat three photos with white cardstock and adhere to a sheet of black cardstock.

step two

Create the title and border strip from stickers.

step three

Attach additional sticker embellishments to the background. Punch a hole in the first eyelet of one of the stickers. String fiber through the hole, a metal-rimmed tag and a jewelry tag. Handwrite onto the tags and finish with chalk.

supplies: Tag: Making Memories; Fiber: Fibers by the Yard; Stickers: Doodlebug Designs Inc.

christmas morning

Designer: Sam Cousins

lincoln

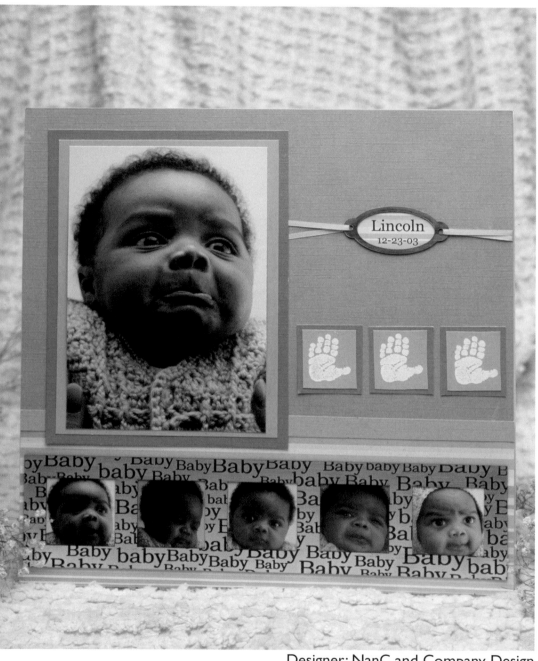

Designer: NanC and Company Design

step one

Cut stripe patterned paper and adhere to the bottom of a sheet of blue cardstock.

step two

Double mat a photo and adhere to the background. Print the name and date of birth of the child onto a piece of stripe patterned paper, cut and fit behind a metallic bookplate. Attach to the background with ribbon.

step three

Adhere five photos behind a metallic filmstrip and adhere to the bottom of the page.

step four

Stamp and heat emboss three pieces of cardstock. Cut into 1¼-inch squares, mat and adhere to the background.

supplies: Cardstock: DCWV; Patterned Paper: DCWV; Metallic Frames: DCWV; Stamp: Inkadinkado; Embossing Powder: Ranger Industries, Inc.

step one

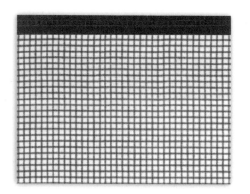

Trim red check patterned paper and adhere to a sheet of denim patterned paper.

step two

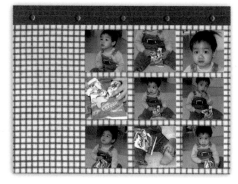

Punch out nine photos with a two-inch square punch and adhere to the background in three rows. Attach five silver snaps to the strip of denim paper.

step three

Print journaling onto cardstock, draw a black line around the journaling block for a border and attach to the background with photo corners. Finish by adhering tile letters to the background for the child's name and a 3D alphabet sticker to the journaling block.

supplies: Patterned Paper: Memories in the Making; Snaps: Making Memories; Tile Letters: Doodlebug Designs Inc; Stickers: Colorbok; Punch: Marvy Uchida; Font: Times New Roman

content

Content [kən-tént]
(adj) quietly
satisfied and
happy: reasonably
happy and satisfied
with the way
things are.

My dear little
Andrew, you are
such a treasure. It
doesn't take much to
make you happy and
content. With a bag
of Goldfish all to
yourself, who needs
anything else, right?
We love you,
Andrew.

andrew

Designer: Leah Fung

blossom festival

JUL 1997
BLOSSOM FESTIV
MOMMY &
JAKE

'I have the happiness
of the passing moment...
what more can a mother ask?'

Designer: Camille Jensen

step one

Cut a piece of blue cardstock to 6¾ x 8¼ inches and adhere to a sheet of stripe patterned paper in the top left corner. Cut a piece of mesh to just shy of 12 inches square and adhere to the background over the blue square.

step two

Triple mat a photo and adhere to the background over the blue square.

step three

Print journaling onto a piece of white cardstock and quadruple mat at an angle. Adhere to the bottom right corner of the background. Adhere a sheer, orange ribbon horizontally across the top of the page.

step four

Handwrite the title and stamp the date onto a piece of green patterned paper. Adhere behind a metallic circle tag and attach to the background with an orange brad as shown.

supplies: Cardstock: DCWV; Patterned Paper: Made to Match; Metal Tag: DCWV; Mesh: Magenta Rubber Stamps; Stamp: Making Memories

20

step one

step two

step three

Cut a strip of green patterned paper and adhere horizontally to the bottom of a sheet of green cardstock. Cut a strip of white textured paper and adhere to the right side of the green cardstock. Cut a piece of red cardstock and adhere over the white strip of paper in the top right corner. Mat a large photo with red cardstock and adhere to the background. Adhere two more photos onto the white strip of paper.

Use rub-ons for the title and key words. Punch three mini squares in the bottom right corner of the large photo.

Tie ribbon through the holes in the photo and attach a bookplate over a portion of the title with brads. Complete the layout with handwritten words and the date.

supplies: Cardstock: Memories in the Making; Patterned Paper: Memories in the Making; Bookplate: Making Memories; Rub-ons: Creative Imaginations; Punch: Fiskars, Inc.

life is good

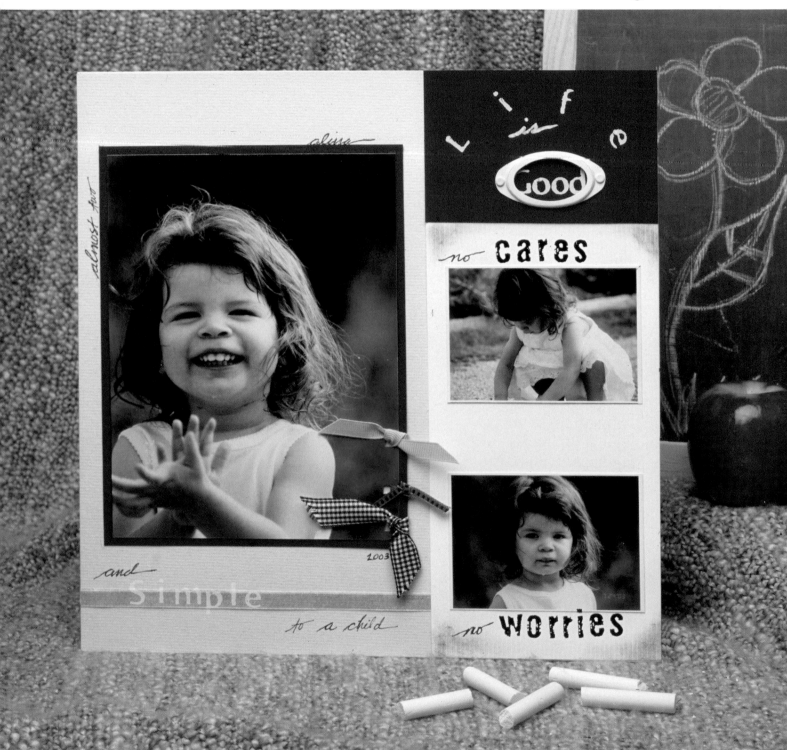

Designer: Anna Estrada Davison

look snow

Look Snow!

Michaela's first view of snow came at Grandma's house. She stared out the window in awe for the longest time. This California girl did not know what to make of all that white stuff.

Designer: Tracy Weinzapfel Burgos

step one

Tear and curl the edges of two pieces of red patterned paper and adhere to a sheet of black cardstock as shown.

step two

Stitch along the edges of the red patterned paper with white thread.

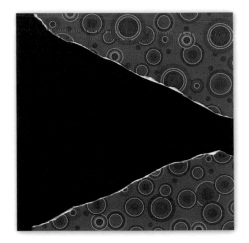

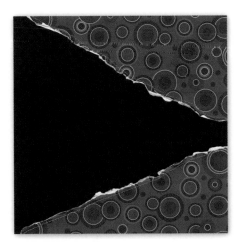

step three

Adhere a photo to the background, trimming and tucking the bottom right corner under the torn edge of the red patterned paper.

step four

Stamp the title onto a piece of white cardstock, frame with a metallic tag, adorn with fibers and adhere to the top right corner of the photo. Print the journaling onto a sheet of vellum. Tear around the edges and attach to the background with white eyelets.

supplies: Cardstock: DCWV; Patterned Paper: DCWV; Metallic Tag: DCWV; Fiber: Fibers by the Yard

20

step one

Mat one photo with blue paper and adhere both photos to the background paper as shown.

step two

Ink the edges of the background paper. Trim a paint chip, mat with blue paper and attach to the background with colored staples.

step three

Attach letter stickers for the title and an epoxy sticker onto the paint chip to highlight the color name. Attach sticker strips over the bottom of the tilted photo. Trace around the colorful letter stickers with a black pen.

step four

Handwrite journaling onto the striped portion of the background. Adhere blue fiber and a carriage charm to the page and complete the layout with word and star stickers.

supplies: Patterned Paper: SEI; Fiber: Fibers by the Yard; Stickers: SEI, Me & My Big Ideas, NRN Designs, Creative Imaginations; Staples: Making Memories

cinderella's castle

Designer: Sam Cousins

my brother

Designer: Tarri Botwinski

step one

Cut two large strips of paper, one from stripe patterned paper and the other from check patterned paper. Adhere the check patterned paper to the top of the mauve cardstock as shown. Adhere the stripe patterned paper to the bottom of the background adhering only the sides and bottom to create a pocket. Double mat a photo and adhere to the top right corner of the background.

step two

Ask a child to handwrite his/her name and age onto a pre-made tag and adhere the tag to the bottom right corner of the background. Adhere a pre-made oval tag to the top left corner for the title.

step three

Print journaling onto paper, cut into tag shapes, ink the edges and attach pre-made oval tags to the top of the journaling tags with snaps.

step four

Slide the tags into the pocket.

supplies: Cardstock: Chatterbox, Inc.; Patterned Paper: Chatterbox, Inc.; Tags: Chatterbox, Inc.; Fibers: Fibers by the Yard; Tacks: Chatterbox, Inc.; Titles: Chatterbox, Inc.; Pen: Marvy Uchida; Ink: ColorBox by Clearsnap, Inc.; Font: Mom's Typewriter

step one

Tear the bottom right corner and the left side of a sheet of black cardstock. Adhere the black cardstock to a sheet of pink patterned paper.

step two

Double mat a photo and adhere to the background as shown. Tear the edges of a vellum quote and ink with black ink. Attach to the bottom right corner of the background with black mini brads.

step three

Thread two gingham ribbons through a ribbon charm and adhere to the left side of the background as shown.

step four

Cut a strip of black mesh. Attach metallic circle letters to the mesh with mini safety pins for the title. Finish the title by attaching pink letter stickers to the mesh.

supplies: Cardstock: DCWV; Patterned Paper: Memories in the Making; Metal Letters: Making Memories; Saftey Pins: Making Memories; Ribbon Charm: Making Memories; Ribbon: Making Memories; Stamps: Making Memories; Templates: QuicKutz; Font: Gigi

my girl

My Girl

My dear Michaela, you'll always be just a little girl to me.

May all your hopes and dreams come true and love fill the days for you.

SEP 2003

Designer: Tracy Weinzapfel Burgos

daughters

Designer: Camille Jensen

20

step one

step two

step three

Cut a piece of orange cardstock to 10½ inches square. Choose a font color a few shades darker than the cardstock and print the word 'daughter' onto the orange cardstock. Turn the orange cardstock 90 degrees and run it through the printer once more to have the word 'daughter' printed onto the cardstock again. Mat the orange cardstock with pink cardstock and adhere to a sheet of floral patterned paper.

Trim four photos and adhere to the underside of an overlay. Triple mat the overlay and adhere to the bottom left corner of the background.

Print journaling onto pink cardstock and tear the edges. Double mat with torn cardstock and adhere to the bottom right corner. Stamp the date onto a piece of orange cardstock and mat with mesh and pink cardstock. Adhere to the background at an angle as shown.

supplies: Cardstock: DCWV; Patterned Paper: Karen Foster Design; Overlay: DCWV; Mesh: Magenta Rubber Stamps; Stamp: Making Memories

step one

Print journaling onto a sheet of beige patterned paper. Trim the beige patterned paper and adhere to a sheet of brown cardstock.

step two

Tear four pieces of three different patterned papers. Adhere the papers in a collage onto the background as shown, being sure not to cover the journaling.

supplies: Patterned Paper: Memories in the Making; Rivets: Chatterbox, Inc.; Letter Embellishment: Li'l Davis Designs

step three

Cut a strip and two corners of faux suede paper. Adhere the strip to the left side of the background. Attach three rivets down the strip. Adhere the two corners to the right corners of the background. Zigzag stitch the edges of the faux suede with brown thread.

step four

Mat a photo with black cardstock. Adhere to the background over a pre-made frame that is set at an angle. Adhere a dominoes piece overlapping the photo and a 3D letter sticker as the first letter of the journaling.

a son is a gift

A son is a gift that makes its presence known, to the thankful heart of a parent, each and every day

Anna Tafoya

Designer: Leah Fung

we love our uncle

Designer: Camille Jensen

step one

step two

step three

Cut a 1-inch strip of yellow cardstock and adhere horizontally to the top of a sheet of stripe patterned paper. Cut a 2½ x 2¾ inch piece of red cardstock and adhere to the bottom right corner of the background. Double mat one photo and triple mat the other and adhere to the background as shown. Cut small strips of the background patterned paper and adhere to the bottom right corner of the photos.

Print the title and journaling onto a transparency.

Attach the transparency to the top of the page with two large blue brads. Stamp the date on mini white tags and attach the tags to the corners of the photos through the transparency with large blue brads.

supplies: Cardstock: DCWV; Patterned Paper: Memories in the Making; Brads: Making Memories; Stamp: Making Memories

step one

Tear strips of blue patterned paper into random sizes. Crumple and ink the paper and adhere to a sheet of white cardstock. Ink the edges of the white cardstock and trim the patterned paper pieces to the edge of the background paper.

step two

Tear the edges of four photos. Adhere, overlapping one another onto the blue patterned paper as shown. Trim any photo that is over the edge of the background paper.

step three

Handwrite onto a journaling tag and attach letter stickers and mini gold brads.

step four

Adhere the journaling tag to the background as shown. Ink a definition and adhere to the background. Attach stickers and an airplane charm with a mini gold brad.

supplies: Patterned Paper: Memories in the Making; Stickers: NRN Designs, Me & My Big Ideas; Punch Out: Memories in the Making; Definition: Making Memories

our frequent flyer

Designer: Sam Cousins

issac

ISSAC

This was not beginner's luck

Designer: NanC and Company Design

step one

step two

step three

Tear the top and bottom and trim the sides of a sheet of green cardstock. Adhere to a sheet of circle patterned paper.

Mat photos with stripe patterned paper and mat a vellum quote with green cardstock. Adhere all to the background.

Cut strips of patterned vellum and adhere to the background in a crisscross pattern. Decoratively stitch the ends of the vellum with black floss. Embellish the layout with letter stickers, 3D stickers, buttons and string.

supplies: Cardstock: DCWV; Patterned Paper: DCWV; Patterned Vellum: Memories in the Making; Buttons: Making Memories; Stickers: Memories in the Making; 3D Stickers: Jolee's Boutique; Floss: Making Memories

step one

Tear a strip of stripe patterned paper and adhere to the left side of a sheet of blue cardstock. Tear a 4 x 5 inch and a 1½ x 4½ inch piece of square patterned paper. Adhere the larger piece to the top right corner and the smaller piece to the bottom left corner of the background.

step two

Triple mat a photo and adhere to the background as shown. Attach letter and dot stickers vertically to the strip of stripe patterned paper for the title.

step three

Tear the edges of a vellum quote, ink with green ink and adhere to the background. Tear a small square of mica and attach to the background overlapping the vellum quote with a decorative square brad.

step four

Tear a square of the square patterned paper and attach to the top left corner of the background with a decorative square brad. Adhere a metallic word onto another torn piece of mica and adhere, overlapping the torn square. Cut two 1-inch squares of mica in half diagonally and adhere to the four corners of the photo.

supplies: Cardstock: Bazzill; Patterned Paper: Memories in the Making, Fresh Prints by The C-Thru Ruler Company; Brads: Making Memories; Stickers: Memories in the Making; Vellum Quote: Fresh Verse by The C-Thru Ruler Company; Mica Pieces: Altered Pages; Ink: Stampin' Up

brothers

friends

brothers

YOU are part of all that surrounds you. Celebrate your connection to the beauty and mystery of Life.
Flavia

Designer: Susan Stringfellow

crying eyes

Designer: NanC and Company Design

step one

Cut brown cardstock into a square and adhere to the bottom right corner of a sheet of tan cardstock.

step two

Adhere a thick strip of check patterned paper and a thin strip of red cardstock to the background, crisscrossing as shown.

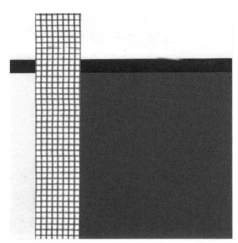

step three

Mat photos with white cardstock and adhere to the background. Cut another thin strip of red cardstock and adhere to the background over the check patterned paper. Stitch the red strips of cardstock with cream floss. Create the title with rub-on letters.

step four

Decorate the edges of a red oval tag with a black pen. Thread a ribbon charm with ribbon, tie around the tag and adhere to the background. Sand metallic hearts and thread wire through the holes of metallic squares. Adhere buttons onto the hearts and the hearts onto the metallic squares.

supplies: Cardstock: DCWV; Patterned Paper: Memories in the Making; Floss: Making Memories; Ribbon Charm: Making Memories; Ribbon: Making Memories; Wire: Artistic Wire Ltd.

step one

Tear strips of orange and purple patterned paper and adhere horizontally to the bottom of a sheet of black cardstock as shown.

step two

Cut a 6½ x 7 inch piece of white cardstock, print journaling on the bottom 2 inches of the shorter side. Chalk certain words and ink the cardstock. Adhere a photo above the journaling, chalk around the photo and draw a line around the photo as a border. Attach spider stickers to the photo. Adhere another photo without matting onto the cardstock as shown. Tear orange and purple patterned paper and adhere to the corners of the photos.

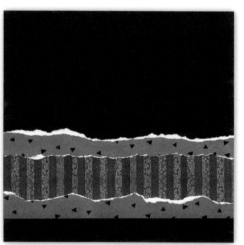

step three

Mat stickers with white cardstock, chalk and ink and adhere to the background onto the purple strip of paper.

step four

Create the title from letter stickers matted with white cardstock. Print child's name and date onto white cardstock. Chalk and ink the white cardstock before adhering to the background.

supplies: Patterned Paper: Memories in the Making; Stickers: Memories in the Making; Pens: ZIG by EK Success; Font: Chatterbox, Inc. Kellys Pen

You don't scare me, little Ms. Witch. However, we did think you were the cutest Halloween witch we ever saw. Your favorite part of the costume was the press on finger nails with spider webs designs. You said you had to make a scary face for the camera. Silly girl, actually mom loved the socks with your fancy black shoes. Every witch needs that extra touch of class especially at the age of eight years old.

SCARY

Brianne – Halloween 2003

Designer: Tonia Boucha

our family

our family

LOVE

Love Love Love Love Love Love Love Love

the cousins

February 2004

Designer: Sam Cousins

step one

Tear the top right corner of a word overlay. Ink the edges of the overlay including the openings for the letters.

step two

Tear a strip of pink patterned paper and cut a square of the pink patterned paper for the corner. Crumple, sand and ink both papers and adhere the strip to the overlay below the openings for the letters and adhere the square behind the torn corner as shown. Trim and adhere photos behind the letter openings of the word overlay.

step three

Adhere four square embellishments to the top left corner of the background with pop dots. Wrap pink fiber underneath them and adhere a letter "C" on top. Tuck two embellishments into the torn corner on the right side of the page. Attach letter stickers for the title above the photos. Attach metallic letters with mini silver brads and letter stickers for the name. Stamp the date below the name. Adhere a ribbon horizontally across the page with a bow as shown.

supplies: Patterned Paper: DCWV; Word Overlay: DCWV; Fiber: Fibers by the Yard; Metallic Letters: DCWV; Brads: Making Memories; Stickers: Chatterbox, Inc., Sonnets by Creative Imaginations; Ribbon: Impress Rubber Stamps; Fresh Cuts: Rebecca Sower; Stamp: Making Memories

step one

Ink the edges and middle of a sheet of beige cardstock with brown ink. Cut a 4½ x 11 inch piece of denim patterned paper. Crumple and adhere to the right side of the background. Cut a 3/4 x 9 inch piece of red patterned paper. Distress the paper with sandpaper and thread through a cork belt buckle. Adhere horizontally to the bottom of the background as shown.

step two

Cut a 6 x 7¾ inch piece of brown textured paper. Tear the lower edge and rub the surface with brown ink and bronze metallic rub-ons. Adhere to the layout as shown.

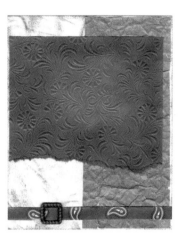

step three

Double mat a photo with red and beige cardstock. Tear the lower edge of the beige cardstock and ink the edges with brown ink. Adhere the photo to the background. Roughly cut out a horse image and rub with brown ink. Adhere to the background over a strip of brown mesh. Adhere a cowboy hat charm overlapping the mesh and horse image.

step four

Adhere cork letters for the title. Print journaling onto a transparency and trim. Cut three 5-inch lengths of brown fiber and braid. Attach the transparency and braided fibers to the background with pewter mini brads through jean button die cuts as shown.

supplies: Cardstock: Bazzill; Patterned Paper: Memories in the Making; Fiber: Fibers by the Yard; Brads: Making Memories; Diecuts: Memories in the Making; Charm: Memories in the Making; Cork Embellishments: Lazerletterz; Horse Image: Altered Pages; Ink: Stampin' Up, Craf-T Products; Transparency: 3M Stationary

go western susie

When I was 9 years old, I took Western riding lessons at Lakeway. My horse was named Chili, and I remember thinking he was just the greatest.

Lake Travis   1973

Designer: Susan Stringfellow

page templates

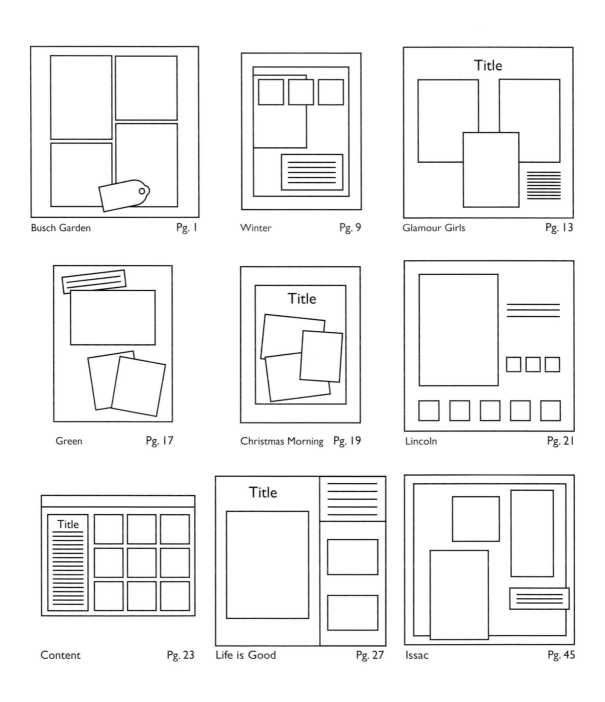

sources

3M Stationary
(800) 364-3577
3m.com

Altered Pages
alteredpages.com

American Crafts
(800) 879-5185
americancrafts.com

Artistic Wire Ltd.
(630) 530-7567
artisticwire.com

Bazzill
(480) 558-8557
bazzillbasics.com

Carolee's Creations
(435) 563-1100
caroleescreations.com

Chatterbox, Inc.
(888) 416-6260
chatterboxinc.com

Clearsnap, Inc.
(800) 448-4862
clearsnap.com

Colorbok
(800) 366-4660
colorbok.com

Craf-T Products
(800) 530-3410
craf-tproducts.com

Creative Imaginations
(800) 942-6487
cigift.com

C-Thru Ruler Company, The
(800) 243-8419
cthruruler.com

DCWV
(801) 224-6766
diecutswithaview.com

Doodlebug Designs Inc.
(801) 966-9952
timelessmemories.ca

Dress It Up!
dressitup.com

EK Success
(800) 524-1349
eksuccess.com

Fibers by the Yard
fibersbytheyard.com

Fiskars, Inc.
(715) 842-2091
fiskars.com

Impress Rubber Stamps
(206) 901-9101
impressrubberstamps.com

Inkadinkado
(781) 938-6100
inkadinkado.com

Jolee's Boutique
joleesbyyou.com

Junkitz
junkitz.com

Karen Foster Design
(001) 451-9779
karenfosterdesign.com

Lasting Impressions
lastingimpressions.safeshopper.
com

LazerLetterz
lazerletterz.com

Li'l Davis Designs
(949) 838-0344
lildavisdesigns.com

Magenta Rubber Stamps
magentarubberstamps.com

Making Memories
(800) 286-5263
makingmemories.com

Marvy Uchida
(800) 541-5877
uchida.com

Me & My Big Ideas
(949) 589-4607
meandmybigideas.com

Memories in the Making
(800) 643-8030
leisurearts.com

NRN Designs
nrndesigns.com

Offray & Son, Inc.
offray.com

Provo Craft
(888) 577-3545
provocraft.com

QuicKutz
(888) 702-1146
quickutz.com

Ranger Industries
(800) 244-2211
rangerink.com

Rebecca Sower
mississippipaperarts.com

Sarah Heidt Photo Craft
(734) 424-2776
sarahheidtphotocraft.com

SEI
(800) 333-3279
shopsei.com

Stampin' Up
(800) 782-6787
stampinup.com

Sticker Studio
stickerstudio.com

upcoming books

look for these published or soon to be published leisure arts scrapbooking idea books

It's All In
Your Imagination

It's All About Baby

It's All About School

It's All About Technique

It's All About
Cards and Tags

It's All About Mini Albums

It's All About
Travel and Vacation

It's All About
Pets and Animals